A PRACTICAL ENGLISH GR

Exercises 9

FUTURE FORMS AND REPO

A. J. THOMSON & A. V. MARTINET

LONDON

OXFORD UNIVERSITY PRESS

*Oxford University Press, Ely House, London W*1

GLASGOW NEW YORK TORONTO MELBOURNE WELLINGTON
CAPE TOWN IBADAN NAIROBI DAR ES SALAAM LUSAKA ADDIS ABABA
DELHI BOMBAY CALCUTTA MADRAS KARACHI LAHORE DACCA
KUALA LUMPUR SINGAPORE HONG KONG TOKYO

ISBN 0 19 432749 3

© Oxford University Press 1972

First published 1972
Second impression 1974

Preface

These exercises are based on chapters 18 and 28 of the authors'
Practical English Grammar.

The exercises on future forms cover much the same ground as
Exercises 2, but there is more emphasis on the contrast between Will
(used for intention at the moment of decision) and the Present
Continuous (used when the intended action is referred to afterwards).
There is also more emphasis on the use of the ordinary future tense
(Will/Shall) as shown in section 201 of the Grammar (2nd edition).
The exercises on indirect speech cover much the same ground as
Exercises 6, but there is more emphasis on the colloquial reporting
of requests and advice. Students are, for example, encouraged to
report such sentences as: 'Would you open the door, please,' said Jack
by: Jack asked me to open the door and 'Could I speak to Tom,
please,' said Ann by: Ann asked to speak to Tom or: Ann asked for
Tom.

All the exercises are moderately difficult, so no grading system is
used.

A key is provided.

This is one of ten booklets based on the above-mentioned Grammar.

Set by Gloucester Typesetting Co. Ltd, Gloucester.
Printed in Great Britain at the University Press, Oxford
by Vivian Ridler Printer to the University

1 The Present Continuous and the Future Tense

[Sections 195, 201]

Put the verbs into the correct tense.

1 Tom: Where you (go) for your next holiday? (= where have you arranged to go?)
Ann: I don't know yet but we probably (go) to Spain.

2 We (have) a drink with Peter tonight (= he has invited us). It's his last night; he (leave) tomorrow.

3 Ann: Do you think we (see) Bill tomorrow?
Mary: I hope so. He probably (look) in on his way to the airport.

4 I (see) my bank manager tomorrow. (= I have arranged this) I'm going to ask him for a loan but I expect he (refuse).

5 I (know) the result tomorrow. As soon as I hear, I (tell) you.

6 Jack's mother: Jack (be) ready in a moment. He is just finishing breakfast.
Jack's father: If I wait for him any longer I (miss) my train. I think I (walk) on; he probably (catch) me up.

7 I probably (come) to London some time next month. I (give) you a ring nearer the time and tell you when I (come). (= when I have decided/arranged to come)

8 Hotel Porter: You (get) a parking ticket if you leave your car there, sir. If you (stay) the night (= have arranged to stay) you (have to) put it in the hotel garage.
Tourist: All right. I (move) it as soon as I've arranged about a room.

9 Ann: I've scorched Bill's shirt. Whatever he (say)?
Mary: Oh, he (not mind). He just (buy) another shirt. He has plenty of money.

10 Peter: We'd better leave a message for Jack. Otherwise he (not know) where we've gone.
George: All right. I (leave) a note on his table.

11 Jack: I don't want to get married. I never (get) married.
Mother: You think that now. But one day you (meet) a girl and you (fall) in love.

12 Tom: I (go) to York tomorrow. (= have arranged to go)
Ann: You (come) back the same day? (= have you arranged to come back?)
Tom: No. I probably (have) to spend the night there.

13 Peter: You (walk) home? (= have you decided to walk?)
   Andrew: Yes. It's too late for a bus.
   Peter: But it's pouring. You (get) soaked! Here, take this um-
   brella.
   Andrew: Thanks very much. I (bring) it back tomorrow.

14 Jack: I (have) another window put in. (= I have arranged this)
   They (start) work on it tomorrow.
   Ann: That (make) the room much brighter.

15 You (take) any exams this term? (= have you decided to take an
   exam?)
   Yes, I (take) an English exam at the end of the month.
   Do you think you (pass)?
   I don't know. If I don't, I (take) it again at the end of next term.

16 Where you (meet) Tom? (= where have you arranged to meet
   him)
   We (meet) at Covent Garden. He (take) me to see *The Magic Flute*.

17 What you (do) next weekend? (= what plans have you made?)
   It depends on the weather. If it's fine we (go) somewhere in the
   car; if it's wet we probably (stay) at home.

18 When Jack (arrive)? (= when did he say he'd arrive?)
   Some time this evening.
   And how he (get) here? (= how has he arranged to travel?)
   I don't know yet. I suppose he (come) by car.

19 What they (do) for their holidays? (= have they decided to do?)
   They (go) camping.
   And what (happen) to their dog? (= what plans have they made
   for the dog?)
   They (take) the dog with them. I think he (enjoy) it more than
   they will.

20 Don't make a sound or you (wake) the baby; and then he (not
   get) to sleep again.

21 Mary: Don't forget that Tom's four boys (spend) the weekend
   here. I don't know how we (manage) with four boys under our
   feet in this small house.
   Jack: I have an idea. We (turn) the attic into a playroom. Then
   they (be able) to play trains without tripping anyone up.

22 Tom: Peter's just phoned to say that he (catch) (= has arranged
   to catch) the 8.10 train and (be) here by 9.0.

23 When George (come) out of hospital? (= what date has been
   fixed?)
   I don't know. They (move) him (= have arranged to move) to

the County Hospital next week so I (have) to ask them about coming out dates.

24 I (ring) Peter tonight (= we have arranged this). I (ask) him to ring you?

No, don't bother. I (be) away most of the week. I (write) to him (*not a previous decision*).

25 Don't worry about meals tomorrow. Everything's been arranged. We (have) breakfast on the train, we (lunch) with the manager— he (stand) us lunch,—and the Smiths (give) us dinner after the show.

26 Tom (*who has just dropped his key on the path*): Never mind; Mary's at home. She (let) us in and we (find) the key tomorrow when it's light.

27 George and Lucy (get) married next week. You (go) to the wedding?

No, I wasn't invited. They (have) a big wedding?

28 I (wait) for you?

No, don't bother. This (take) a long time, I'm sure, and I don't want you to miss your train.

29 Tom, the host: What you (have), Paul?

Paul: I (have) the grilled steak, please.

Tom: And I (have) roast duck. (*He gives his orders to the waiter and then studies the wine list*): Hm. You (have) steak and I (have) duck. We (have) some red wine.

30 Jack: I (give) you a lift to work tomorrow if you like.

Tom: Have you borrowed a car?

Jack: No, I've just bought one. I (collect) it this afternoon.

31 Ann: Peter has set his alarm clock for 5 a.m. He (get) up very early, isn't he?

Mother: Early! Do you know what (happen)? The alarm bell (ring), Peter (sleep) through it and he (come) down to breakfast at the usual time or a little later.

32 Peter: I (be) promoted next week. Mr Jones (leave) and I (take) over the department (*these arrangements have already been made*).

Ann: At this rate you soon (be) a director, and then you (spend) two hours a day on business lunches and (lose) your figure.

33 Tom: I (fly) to New York next week (*this has been arranged*).

Jack: You (take) your wife with you?

Tom: No. I know that if I take her she (spend) all her time and most of my money in the New York shops.

34 Mary: Jack and I (go) out tonight. We (have) dinner at the
   Festival Hall and (go) to a concert afterwards.
   Ann: And what about the children? I (come) and babysit if you like.
   Mary: Oh, my neighbour (come) in to sit with them. But thank
   you for offering, Ann. I (ask) you next time.

35 Nadia: I see that *Lord of the Flies* (come) to our local cinema
   next week.
   George: Oh, good. We (go) and see it together on Monday
   night?
   Nadia: Yes, let's. I (get) the book out of the library and then I
   (be able) to compare the book and the film.
   George: If you do that out loud during the film I (not pay) for
   your supper afterwards.

36 Ann (*reading newspapers*): It says here that Smiths (open) their
   new department next week, and that they (have) a sale to give it a
   good start. I think I (look) in on Monday at lunchtime.
   Mary: Good idea! I (come) too.
   Peter (*entering room*): Where you girls (have) lunch today?
   Mary: We (miss) lunch. We (go) to a sale instead.

2 Present Continuous and Going To

[Sections 195, 198]

Put the verbs in brackets into one of the above forms.

1 Where you (go) for your holidays?   I (go) to Norway.
  What you (do) there?   I (fish).
2 Where you (go) this evening?
  I (not go) anywhere. I (stay) at home. I (write) some letters.
3 Take an umbrella; it (rain).
4 How long you (stay) in this country? (= how long have you
  decided to stay?)
  Another month. I (go) home at the end of the month.
  What you (do) then?
  I (try) to get a job.
5 I (dye) these curtains.
  You (do) it yourself, or (have) it done?
  I (have) it done. Who should I take them to?

6 I've seen the film, now I (read) the book. I've just got a copy from the library. (I haven't started the book yet.)

7 You (do) anything next weekend?
Yes, my nephews (come) and I (show) them round London.
You (take) them to the theatre? (= have you booked seats?)
No, they're too young for that. I (take) them to the Zoo.

8 We (start) early tomorrow. We (go) to Ben Nevis.
You (climb) Ben Nevis?
Not me. Tom (climb) it. I (sit) at the bottom and (do) some sketching.

9 Uncle: I hear you (go) to the Zoo tomorrow. You (feed) the bears?
Niece: No, but we (take) our cameras. We (try) to photograph the animals.

10 You (not ask) your boss to give you a fire in your office?
It isn't worth while. I (leave) at the end of the week.
Really. And what you (do) then? You (have) a holiday?
No, I (start) another job the following Monday.

11 I hear you've bought a caravan. You (use) it for your holidays?
No, I (live) in it. I (start) moving my things next week.
What you (do) with your house?
I (sell) it to the man who sold me the caravan. He (get) married next month.

12 Mrs Jones (go) to hospital. She (have) her appendix out.
Who (look) after the children?
Her sister (come) down from Scotland.

13 He isn't happy at his boarding school. I (send) him to a day school.
Have you decided on the other school?
No, but I (see) (= have an appointment with) the headmaster of the Park School this afternoon. I'll probably send him there.

14 Tom (arrive) tomorrow.
He (spend) the weekend here or (catch) the night train back as usual?
He (spend) the weekend. He (give) a lecture on Friday and (attend) a big reception on Saturday.

15 He (bring) his wife with him? (= Has he arranged to bring his wife?)
Yes. She (do) some shopping while he (give) his lecture.

16 I've just arranged to do a part-time job. I (start) on Monday.
What you (do) the rest of the time?
I (study).

17 You (go) abroad for your holiday?
No, I (get) a holiday job. I (go) to an agent's on Saturday to find
out about it. I (ask) for a job abroad; but of course they may all
be taken.
You might get a job picking grapes. Jack (join) a camp in the
South of France: his university arranged it; and they all (pick)
grapes.

18 I (buy) a new coat. The weather report says that it (be) very cold.

19 Ann has won a car in a competition but she can't drive.
Tom: What you (do) with the car? You (sell) it?
Ann: No, I (learn) to drive. I (have) my first lesson next Monday.

20 I hear you've bought a new house.
Yes, I (move) in next week.
You (have) a house warming party?
Not just yet. I (paint) the house first. The paint's in a terrible
state.

21 You (have) it done? (= Have you arranged to have it done?)
No, I (do) it myself. I (use) that non-drip paint so it shouldn't
be too difficult. And the family (help), of course.
What about ladders?
Oh, I've fixed that. I (hire) from the local Do-it-Yourself shop.

22 I (do) a lot of work in the garden, too. I (plant) 20 apple trees
and (make) a lawn in front of the house.
All that digging will take years. You (give) up your job?

23 I (get) some help with the garden (= I have arranged this.) Two
men (start) work on the hedge on Friday and a lawn expert
(come) on Monday to advise me about the lawn.

24 The employers (meet) the strikers again tomorrow (= this has
been arranged).
They just (repeat) what they said today? Or they (climb) down?
I believe that they (offer) 10 per cent.

3 Going to and Will + infinitive [Section 202]

Put the verbs in brackets into one of the above forms.

1 Where are you off to with that ladder?
I (have) a look at the roof; it's leaking and I think a tile has
slipped.

2 We bought our new garage in sections and we (assemble) it ourselves.

That sounds rather interesting. I (come) and help you if you like.

3 Why do you want all the furniture out of the room?

Because I (shampoo) the carpet. It's impossible to do it unless you take everything off it first.

4 Here are the matches; but what do you want them for?

I (make) a bonfire at the end of the garden; I want to burn that big heap of rubbish.

Well, be careful. If the fire gets too big it (burn) the apple trees.

5 Have you decided on your colour scheme?

Oh yes, and I've bought the paint. I (paint) this room blue and the sitting room green.

6 Why are you asking everyone to give you bits of material?

Because I (make) a patchwork quilt.

7 I wonder if Ann knows that the time of the meeting has been changed.

Probably not. I (look) in on my way home and tell her. I'm glad you thought of it.

8 Leave a note for them on the table and they (see) it when they come in.

9 I'm afraid I'm not quite ready.

Never mind. I (wait).

10 Do you have to carry so much stuff on your backs?

Yes, we do. We (camp) out and (cook) our own meals, so we have to carry a lot.

11 I've been measuring the windows. I (put) in double glazing.

12 You (wear) that nice dress in a dinghy?

Of course not! I (sit) on the pier and (watch) you all sailing. I (not get) all wet and muddy and pretend that I'm enjoying it!

13 If you leave your keys with the hall porter he (take) the car round to the garage.

14 Shop assistant: We have some very nice strawberries.

Customer: All right. I (have) a pound.

15 Husband: This bread is absolutely tasteless! I wish we could have home-made bread.

Wife: All right. I (start) making it. I (get) a book about home baking today, and from now on I (bake) all our bread!

16 Mary: Ann's busy baking. Apparently she (bake) all their bread from now on.

Jean: She soon (get) tired of that.

17 Why have you brought your camera? You (try) to take photographs? It's not allowed, you know.
No, I (try) to sell the camera.
That's not allowed either. If a policeman sees you, he (confiscate) the camera.

18 Tom to Jack, who has just helped him to change a wheel: I (have) to leave this at the garage; I don't know how to mend a puncture in a tubeless tyre.
Jack: But it's quite easy. I (come) round this evening and show you if you like.

19 Later:
Tom to wife: I (not take) the tyre to a garage. I (mend) it myself. Jack (help) me.

20 Why are you rolling up the carpets? You (paint) the ceiling?
No, I (take) the carpet to the cleaners'.

21 Ann: Here's the letter to the landlord. If there's anything I should add, say so and I (add) it.
Peter: It's fine, but it's illegible. He (not be able) to read it.
Ann: Oh, I (type) it! (= she had always intended to type it)
Peter: Good, then we (have) a copy.

22 Employer: But there are a lot of mistakes in this, Miss Jones.
Miss Jones: Yes, I suppose there are. All right, I (type) it again.

23 Mrs Smith: Your cold's worse, Ann. Go back to bed and I (ring) the school and tell them you can't come.

24 Mrs Smith was just picking up the receiver when her husband came downstairs. 'Ann's not well,' she said. 'I (ring) the school and say that she can't come.'

25 Ann: Why are you taking fishing rods? You (not climb) the mountain after all?
Tom: We (climb) *and* fish. There's a lake on top and we (try) to get some fish out of it.
Ann: Well, if you catch any I (cook) them; but I think I (buy) some all the same.

26 Mary, meeting Jack carrying two buckets of water: Hello, Jack! Where's the fire?
Jack: I (wash) the car, if you want to know. Would you like to help me?
Mary: I'm not dressed for it but I (come) and watch.

27 Where are all those children off to with baskets?
They (pick) blackberries. They probably (come) back at 6.0 with their baskets crammed and then their mothers (start) making jam.

28 Ann: You (have) to go now, Tom, or you (be) late.
   Mary: But it's pouring. He (get) soaked if he goes out in that.
   Tom: You're right. You (let) me stay a little longer?

29 George and Paul find an injured man lying by the roadside.
   Paul: I (stay) with him, George, if you go back and get help.
   George: All right. I (try) to get a lift back.

30 No, I'm not going away for the weekend. I'm staying at home. I
   (start) building my garage. The bricks have come at last.
   You (do) it all by yourself?
   No, my nephew (help) me. I suggested it to him yesterday and
   he was quite enthusiastic.

31 He says he's tired of writing books about horrible people who get
   more and more horrible every page, and now he (write) about
   perfectly charming people who are happily married.
   I wonder if anyone (buy) it.
   Oh yes, people (buy) it. He's a famous writer.

32 I hear the farmer down the road has hired a bulldozer.
   Yes, he (dig) up all his hedges and put in fences instead.

33 The new owner (make) any changes?
   He's made some already. You should see his new menus. He
   (concentrate) more on the restaurant than the shop.

34 What do you want all those corks for?
   I've bought a cask of wine and I (bottle) it myself.

35 There's someone at the door.
   I (go)! But I expect it's someone for you.

36 Where are you all going?
   There's nothing to eat or drink here except one chop and a
   bottle of champagne, so we (buy) some fish and chips and eat
   them in the car. Come with us.
   No, thanks. I think I (stay) and use up the chop and champagne.

4 Future Continuous and Will + infinitive
[Section 208]

Put the verbs in brackets into one of the above forms.

1 Jack usually gives me a lift home, but we both (come) home by
train tomorrow as his car is being repaired.

2 He says he (meet) us at the bus stop, but I'm sure he (forget) to turn up.

3 Don't ring now; she (cook) the children's supper.
All right. I (ring) at 8.30.

4 I wonder what I (do) this time next year.
I expect you still (work) at the same office.

5 I'd like to redecorate the kitchen.
All right. I (get) some paint on Saturday morning and we (do) it this weekend.

6 Wait a bit. Don't drink your tea without milk. The milkman (come) in a minute.

7 What are you doing next weekend?
Oh, I (work) as usual. I'm always on duty at weekends.

8 Air hostess: We (take) off in a few minutes. Please fasten your seat belts.

9 He (come) if you ask him.

10 I arranged to play tennis with Tom at nine tonight.
But you (play) in semi-darkness. You won't be able to see the ball.

11 I (get) you some cigarettes if you like. The shops still (be) open.
No, don't bother. The office boy (go) out in a minute to post the letters; I (ask) him to buy me some.

12 It (be) very late when she gets home and her parents (wonder) what's happened.

13 I never (be) able to manage on my own.
But you won't be on your own. Tom (help) you. Look—his name is bracketed with yours on the list.
Oh, that's all right. But Tom (not help) me: I (help) Tom. He always takes charge when we're on duty together.

14 I (write) postcards every week, I promise, and I (try) to make them legible. If necessary I (type) them.

15 Are you in a hurry for this letter, Mr Jones? Because I (type) Mr White's letters at four o'clock and if yours could wait till—
Mr Jones: I'd like it a little earlier than four if possible.
Typist: All right. I (type) it for you now.

16 What happened at last night's meeting? I hear there was quite a disturbance.
Come and see me and I (tell) you. I don't want to talk about it on the phone.

17 I'm going to Switzerland next week.
You're lucky. The wild flowers just (come) out.

18 This time next month the snow (melt) and skiing will be over.
19 The first day of the term will be horrible, for everybody (talk) about their holidays and (show) photographs of marvellous foreign beaches, and as I haven't been anywhere I (feel) terribly out of it.
20 I (tell) her what you say but she (not believe) it.
21 It's 7 a.m. and here we are on top of a mountain. At home people just (get) up now.
22 But you can't go to a fancy dress party in a dinner jacket! Why not?
Because everyone (wear) fancy dress.
All right. I (wrap) the hearthrug round me and (go) as a caveman.
23 The coming election (be) the main topic of conversation for the next fortnight. The party leaders (speak) on T.V. and the local candidates (address) meetings in the constituencies.
24 This time tomorrow everyone (read) of your success, and all sorts of people (ring) up to congratulate you.
25 That oak tree still (stand) there fifty years from now.
26 You please (forward) my mail to the Grand Hotel? I (stay) there as usual for the first fortnight in August.
27 Heavens! Look at the time. Your father (come) home in a minute and I haven't even started getting dinner ready!
28 James (leave) for Australia quite soon. He has got a job there.
29 The car (not start).
If you get in, Tom and I (give) it a push.
30 It's the middle of December. Carol singers (come) round soon.
31 On the news tonight they mentioned the possibility of a power strike. Everybody (look) for candles tomorrow.
32 Hotel receptionist on phone to client: What time you (arrive), Mr Jones?
Mr Jones: I (travel) on the 4.30 from Victoria. There (be) taxis at the station?
Receptionist: Don't bother about taxis, Mr Jones. We (send) the hotel station wagon down for you.
33 You (use) your dictionary this afternoon?
No. You can borrow it if you like.
Thanks very much. I (put) it back on your desk this evening.
34 Ann: This time next week I (have) my first skiing lesson.
Tom: And this time next month you (lie) in bed with a broken ankle!

35 It's a beautiful drive. I'm sure you (enjoy) the scenery.
   I (not have) a chance to look at it. I (map-read), and Tom gets
   so furious if I make a mistake that I (be) afraid to take my eyes
   off the map.
36 I (write) in code if you insist, but I don't think it's at all
   necessary.

5 Future Continuous
and Will (mostly negative)   [Section 208]

1 You ask him; it's no good my asking him. He (not do) anything I
   say.
2 Ann says she (not come) if Tom is driving. She says she doesn't
   want to die yet.
   Well, tell her Tom (not drive). He's had his licence suspended.
3 Pupil to teacher: I (not come) back next term. My parents want
   me to get a job.
4 Headmaster: I (not have) boys here with long hair, so get your
   hair cut. If you come here tomorrow with long hair I'll send you
   home.
   Boy: All right, I (not come) tomorrow. I'll get a job.
5 Mother: I'm so grateful for the help you've given Jack; I hope
   you'll be able to go on helping him.
   Teacher: I'm afraid I (not teach) him next term because I only
   teach the fifth form and he'll be in the sixth.
6 Schoolboy in school dining hall: The last week of our last term!
   I wonder what we (do) this time next year.
   Friend: Well, we (not eat) school dinners anyway. That's one
   comfort.
7 They give very good dinners at the school but my daughter (not
   eat) them. She prefers to go out and buy fish and chips.
8 Yes, you can stroke the dog; he (not bite) you.
9 Shall we meet him at the station?
   Oh, he (not come) by train. He never comes by train.
10 I've fished that river every year for the last fifteen years.
   Well, nobody (fish) it next year. The water's been polluted. All
   the fish are dead.
11 I'll cook any fish you catch, but I (not clean) them. You'll have
   to do that yourself.

12 I (not show) any films this time. The projector's broken down.
13 Housewife: This time next week I (not wash) up the breakfast things. I (have) breakfast in bed in a luxury hotel.
14 I (not wear) glasses when you see me next. I'll be wearing contact lenses. You probably (not recognise) me.
15 I'll tell him the truth of course. But it (not be) any good. He (not believe) me.
16 Customer: When you deliver my next order—
   Shop assistant: We (not deliver) any more orders, I'm afraid. This branch is closing down.
17 It'll be easy to pick her out in that bright red coat of hers. But she (not wear) the red coat! She's given it away.
18 No, I (not tell) you the end! Go on reading and find out for yourself!
19 You (not use) your car when you're on holiday, will you? No, but don't ask me to lend it to you because I (not do) it. Not after what happened last time.
20 I (have) to be a bit careful about money when I retire because I'll only be getting half my present salary. But of course I (not pay) supertax.
21 You can either pay the fine or go to prison for a month. I (not pay) the fine.
   Then you (have) to go to prison.
22 He's a clever boy but he's lazy. He (not work).
23 I wonder how Jack (get on) with the new secretary. Oh, Jack (not work) here after this week. He's being transferred.
24 According to the brochures this hotel prides itself on its service, but the staff not even (show) a guest to his room unless he insists. I (not come) here again.

6 Future Perfect   [Section 210]

Put the verbs in brackets into the future perfect tense.

1 I hope they (repair) this road by the time we come back next summer.
2 By the end of next week my wife (do) her spring cleaning and we'll all be able to relax again.

3 Yes, I make jam every week. I (make) about 200 lbs. by the end of the summer.

4 In two months' time he (finish) his preliminary training and will be starting work.

5 He spends all his spare time planting trees. He says that by the end of next year he (plant) 2000.

6 I'll be back again at the end of next month.
I hope I (pass) my driving test by then. If I have, I'll meet your train

7 Come back in an hour. I (do) my packing by then and we'll be able to have a talk.

8 When he reaches Land's End he (walk) 1000 miles.

9 He's only 35 but he's started losing his hair already. He (lose) it all by the time he's 50.

10 His father left him £50,000, but he lives so extravagantly that he (spend) it all before he's 30.

11 By the end of next year I (work) for him for 45 years.

12 Everywhere you go in London you see blocks of flats being pulled down and huge hotels being erected. In ten years' time all the private residents (be driven) out and there'll be nothing but one vast hotel after another.

13 Our committee is trying to raise money to buy a new lifeboat. By the end of the year we (send) out 5,000 letters asking for contributions.

14 By the end of my tour I (give) exactly the same lecture 53 times.

15 A hundred people have died of starvation already. By the end of the week two hundred (die). When are you going to send help?

16 Since he began driving, Tom has driven an average of 5,000 miles a year, and had an average of $2\frac{1}{2}$ accidents a year. So by the time he's 60 he (drive) 200,000 miles and had 50 accidents. Let's try to persuade him to go back to cycling.

17 Did you say you wanted help picking apples? I could come on 1st October.
We (pick) them all by then. But come all the same.

18 Apparently Venice is slowly sinking into the sea. Scientists are trying to save it but by the time they've found the answer the city probably (sink).

7 Will and Shall [Sections 199, 200 and Chapter 21]

Insert either **will** or **shall** in the spaces; for the sake of clarity do not contract **shall** or **will** in the affirmatives.

1 I ... know tomorrow. It ... be in the papers.

2 These pigeons are quite tame; they ... take crumbs from your fingers.

3 ... I call for you?
No, I ... get a taxi and meet you at the station.

4 Take these letters to the post, ... you, and shut the door after you!

5 Loudspeaker announcement at an air terminal: '... Mr Jones, passenger to New York, please come to Gate 3.'

6 The Head of the Department has just told me that I ... (not) have any nine o'clock classes next term. So I ... (not) have to get up early, which ... be a comfort. And I ... have time to read the paper at breakfast.

7 Zoo keeper: In spite of all the notices, people ... feed these animals.

8 Extract from official Safety Regulations for theatres: Persons ... not be permitted to stand or sit in the gangways.

9 You can trust me; nobody ... know that you are here. I ... (not) even tell my wife.

10 Shop assistant: The small ones are £1 each and the large ones are £2.
Customer: I ... have six small ones, please.

11 ... we stop here for a drink?
If we do, we ... miss the overture, and they probably ... (not) let us in till the end of the act.

12 ... you have another piece of pie?
Yes, please.

13 Jones: Stand away from that door! You can't keep me here against my will!
Smith: You ... (not) go till you have given me an explanation! (= I won't let you go)

14 Police Officer in a loud-speaker van beside a motorway in thick fog: They are going much too fast. I keep warning them to reduce speed but they ... (not) do it.

15 Extract from a club's regulations: Club officers ... be elected yearly and ... (not) be eligible for re-election at the end of that year.

16 The train ... be very crowded, I'm afraid. I expect we ... have
   to stand most of the way.

17 Ann on phone: You left your gloves here last night. ... I post
   them to you?
   Mary: No, don't bother. I ... pick them up some time this evening. You ... be in, ... (not) you?

18 At the races: Tom: Who won?
   Jack: I don't know; it was a photo-finish. But we ... see in a
   moment. They ... put the winner's number up.

19 Ann: She says she'd rather go to prison than pay the fine.
   Tom: She ... (not) go to prison. (= I won't let this happen.) I
   ... pay her fine for her!

20 Where ... we go to get shoes?
   What about Oxford Street?
   Oxford Street? Are you mad? It's Saturday morning! The shops
   ... be packed.

21 I ... (not) see her, I'm sorry to say. She ... have left by the
   time I arrive.

22 Secretary: There's a Mr Peterson in the outer office, sir. He says
   he has an appointment. ... you see him now?
   Mr Smith: I ... (not) see him now or at any other time. I told
   him so when we last met. And he hasn't an appointment!

23 Angry villagers, who have just heard that the government
   intends to pull down their houses and build an airfield: They
   ... (not) build an airfield here! We ... fight for our village!

24 I am determined that my son ... have the best possible edu-
   cation.

8 Time Clauses   [Section 293]

Put the verbs in brackets into the correct tense.

1 Heat the oil till it (begin) to bubble.
2 I'll stay here till Tom (get) back.
3 We'll go out as soon as the shops (open).
4 You drive first, and when you (be) tired, I'll take over.
5 The sooner we (start), the sooner we'll get there.
6 We will send you the goods as soon as we (receive) your cheque.
7 I'll wait as long as you (like).

8 Whip the whites of the eggs till they (be) quite stiff.

9 Shall I jump out when the bus (slow) down at the next corner?

10 No, you'd better wait till it (stop) at the traffic lights.

11 You are too young to understand. I (explain) it to you when you (be) older.

12 Tom: Brown is the best poet in the university.
   Ann: Now read Smith's poems. When you (read) them you'll say that he is better.

13 Tom: I can't get used to driving on the left.
   Jack: When you (be) here for another week you'll find it quite easy.

14 The room doesn't look particularly attractive now but when I (clean) and (paint) it, it will look quite different.

15 Pour boiling water on the coffee grounds, wait till the grounds (settle), then strain it into a clean jug.

16 As soon as they (see) the river the children will want to bathe.

17 When we (see) the cathedral we'll go to the museum.

18 What will you do when you (finish) painting the bridge?

19 Oh, this bridge is so long that by the time we (reach) the other end it will be time to start again at this end.

20 Serve the meal and wash up. When you (do) the washing up you can go home.

21 The plane won't take off till the fog (lift).

22 Tom will start as soon as his visa (arrive).

23 I'm glad you're learning French. When you (know) French I (give) you a job.

24 Shall I boil the baby's milk?
   Yes, but don't give it to him till it (cool).

25 Don't start smoking till the others (finish) their meal.

26 By the time you (give) the children their meal you won't have any appetite left.

27 I don't want to discuss it over the phone, but I (tell) you about it when I (get) home.

28 How do you like your new job?
   I've only just started so I really can't say. When I (be) in it for a fortnight I (let) you know.

29 Have you flown solo yet?
   No, but my instructor says that when I (fly) another ten hours, he'll let me.

30 They say that when the 70 m.p.h. speed limit (be) in operation for a year, they will be able to judge whether it is effective or not.

31 Sculptor's friend: I suppose that when I (come) back next year you will still be working on this horse.

32 Sculptor: Oh no, I (finish) it long before I (see) you again, but as soon as I (finish) one thing I (start) on another, so there'll be something else for you to look at.

33 All the flats are exactly alike so when you (see) one you've seen them all.

34 Advertisement: When you (drive) a Jaguar once, you won't want to drive another car.

35 He's asleep now but I (give) him the letter as soon as he (wake) up.

36 She bought beer and made sandwiches because she knew that when they (arrive) they would be hungry and thirsty.

9 Time Clauses   [Section 293]

Put the verbs in brackets into the correct tense.

1 When it (get) dark we'll have to stop. We can't work in the dark.

2 Go on till you (come) to a square with a statue in the middle; then turn left and you'll find the theatre on your right.

3 Immediately the train (stop) we'll jump out.

4 I'll help you with your homework as soon as I (do) my own.

5 He was determined to keep the two dogs apart because he knew that the moment they (see) one another they'd start barking furiously.

6 I know the coat's unfashionable but I'm not going to throw it away. I'll keep it till that style (come) into fashion again.

7 Tourist: Can we get to the top of the tower?
Guide: Yes, but be careful when you (go) up because the steps are very uneven.

8 Tourist, puffing up the steps: I'll be glad when I (get) to the top!
Guide: When you (see) the view you'll be glad you made the effort.

9 Mother to child setting out for school: When you (come) to the main road remember to stop and look both ways before you (cross), won't you?

10 'Give this letter to your teacher as soon as you (arrive) at
school,' said his mother.
'All right,' said the boy, running out.
'I bet it will still be in his pocket when he (get) home tonight,'
said his father.

11 Tom: I'm going to New York by sea. I'm leaving tomorrow.
Jack: I'm going by air. When I (sit) in my comfortable plane I'll
think of you tossing about on a stormy sea.
Tom: When I (walk) about the deck enjoying the fresh air and
blue sea I'll think of you shut up in a flying box seeing nothing.

12 But there's someone in the phone box! You can't rush in and
grab the receiver. You'll have to wait till he (finish).

13 The ladder looks a bit unsteady.
Yes, but before he (start) working from it he will tie the top end
to the tree.

14 The house won't be entirely mine until I (pay) off the mortgage.

15 You'll find that the staff will clock in very punctually but that
they won't do any work till the boss (arrive).

16 When I (work) here for fifteen years I'll be entitled to a pension.

17 When you (do) the bedrooms, remember to sweep under the beds.

18 When you (do) all the upstairs rooms, come down and give me a
hand with the lunch.

19 Mother to child: I won't give you any cake until you (eat) your
bread and butter.

20 We'll talk business when we (have) dinner, but not during
dinner. I never talk business at meals.

21 Young man: Weren't you astonished when she said that?
Old man: When you (be) married as long as I have, you won't be
so easily astonished.

22 When you (read) this book, leave it in the hospital for someone
else to read.

23 He said he would give me a ring as soon as he (reach) Paris.

24 Some people say that a man shouldn't think of marrying till he
(save) up enough money to buy a house.

25 You're an idiot to go into teaching. I'm going into business. In
ten years' time when you (queue) at the bus stop I'll be driving
by in my Bentley.

26 When you are picking fruit in the holidays to eke out your
salary I (cruise) round the Greek islands in my private yacht.

27 I visit a new country every year. By the time I (be) sixty I shall
have visited all the countries in the world.

28 When I (see) all there is to see I'll buy a small island and settle down there.

29 He saves £500 a year. By the time he (retire) he'll have saved £5,000.

30 By the time he (save) £5,000, the value of money will have gone down so much that he'll have to go on working.

31 Ann hoped that it would go on raining. She knew that the moment it (stop) Tom would want to go out.

32 I hoped that Jack would be there when the train (arrive), but there was no sign of him.

33 The boys worked slowly for they knew that as soon as they (finish) one exercise the master would tell them to do the next.

34 I'll take the paper with me. I'll read it while I (wait) for the bus.

35 The window-cleaner was in fact one of a gang of safe crackers. He hoped that while he (clean), or (pretend) to clean, windows he would be able to have a look at the safe.

36 He said that he would lend me money whenever I (need) it.

10 Reported Speech: Statements

[Sections 276, 277]

Note applying to all reported speech exercises

When the speaker says **you**, and the person spoken to is not identified, it is good practice for the student to assume that the remark was made to himself. **you** will then become **I/me** or **we/us**. (Answers in the key will be given in first person forms.)
e.g. 'You can phone from my office,' he said.
    He said I could phone from his office.
This must not, of course, be done when the person spoken to is identified.
    'You can phone from my office, Ann,' he said.
    He told Ann that she could phone from his office.
Note that when **you** stands for **one**, it is reported unchanged.
    'You can't bathe in the rivers,' he said, 'they're full of piranhas.'
    He said that you couldn't bathe in the rivers as they were full of piranhas.

Put the following statements into indirect speech.

1 'I'm going out now, but I'll be in by nine,' he said. (*Omit* **now**)

2 'I'm working in a restaurant, and don't much care for it,' she said.

3 'I can't live on my basic salary,' said Peter. 'I'll have to offer to do overtime.'

4 'My young brother wants to be a tax inspector,' said Mary. 'I can't think why. None of my family has ever been a tax inspector.'

5 'We're waiting for the school bus,' said the children. 'It's late again.'

6 'I've made a terrible mistake!' said Peter.
'You're always making terrible mistakes,' I said. 'You should be used to it by now.'

7 'We make £50 a week,' said one of the men, 'and send most of it home to our wives.'

8 'It's lonely being away from our families,' said another, 'but we earn three times as much in this factory as we would in our own country.'

9 'We've been here for two and a half years,' said the man who had spoken first, 'and we're going to stay another six months.'

10 'I've got a job on an oil-rig,' said Paul.
'That'll be very hard work,' I said.
'I know it'll be hard,' he replied, 'but I don't mind hard work, and it'll be good experience.'

11 'The ice will soon be hard enough to skate on,' said Tom.
'I'll look for my skates when I get home,' Ann said.

12 'I'm living with my parents at present,' she said, 'but I hope to have a flat of my own shortly.'

13 'I'm leaving tomorrow,' she said, 'by the 4.30 from Victoria.'
'We'll come and see you off,' we said.

14 'I've just bought a car,' said Peter, 'but it's not insured yet so I can't take you for a drive.'

15 'I'd like to come to the phone,' said Mary, 'but I'm bathing the babies and they will drown if I leave them alone in the bath.'

16 Mary has just received a postcard from Ann, beginning, 'I'm coming up to London next week. I hope you and Jack will meet me for lunch one day.' (*Imagine that Mary is reading this card to Jack. Begin: Ann says . . .*)

17 'Nothing ever happens in the village,' she said. 'It's like a dead village. All the young people have gone away.'

18 'I've missed my train,' said Bill. 'Now I'll be late for work and my boss will be furious.'

19 'We'll wait for you if you're late,' they said.

20 'They are supposed to be landing at London airport,' I said. 'But if the fog gets any thicker the plane may be diverted.'

21 'If you lend me the book,' said Mary, 'I'll bring it back the day after tomorrow.'

22 'I hate getting up on these dark mornings,' grumbled Peter. 'It is horrible,' agreed his wife, 'but the mornings will be lighter soon and then it won't be quite so bad.'

23 'The sales are starting tomorrow,' said the typist. 'As soon as we finish work the whole typing pool is going to make a dash for the shops.'
'I hope you'll all get what you want,' I said.

24 'I wish I had something to eat,' said Peter.
'You've only just had lunch,' said his sister. 'I don't know how you can be hungry again so soon.'

25 'If you're short of money I can lend you £50,' said my aunt, 'and you can take your time about paying it back.'

26 'I usually take my dog out for a walk when I come home from work,' he said.

27 'I have a message for your brother,' I said.
'He isn't at home,' said Ann. 'He left two days ago.'

28 'I bought this hat in Milan,' I said.
'You shouldn't have bought that colour,' said Peter. 'It doesn't go with your coat.'

29 'I must hurry. My father is always furious if any of us are late for meals,' she said.

30 'If you want to smoke you'll have to go upstairs,' said the bus conductor.

31 'I'm building myself a house,' said Charles. 'I won't show it to you just yet but when the roof is on you can come and see it.'

32 'The lake will probably freeze tonight,' said Peter. 'It's much colder than last night.'
'I'll go out and look early in the morning,' said Mary, 'and if it's frozen I'll make some holes in the ice so that the ducks can feed.'

33 'Even if the strikers go back to work tomorrow it will be some time before things return to normal,' said the official.

34 'Someone is trying to murder me!' said Mrs Jones. 'I keep getting threatening letters.'

35 'I'm taking my children to the zoo tomorrow,' she said, 'to see the baby polar bear.'

36 'All I can hear,' says Ann, 'is a high-pitched buzz. I wonder if it's some sort of signal.'

11 Reported Speech: Statements

[Sections 276, 277]

(i) See note to exercise 10.

(ii) **Had better**

'**You'd better**' can be reported unchanged (though the pronoun may change) but can also be reported by **advise**:

He said, 'You'd better tell Tom' He said I'd better tell Tom.
  He advised me to tell Tom.

'**I/we had better**' will normally be reported unchanged (though the pronoun may change):

He said, 'I'd better wait.' He said he'd better wait.

(iii) '**I should . . . (if I were you)**' is best reported by **advise**:

I said, 'Shall I write to Ann?'
'I should phone her (if I were you),' said Peter.
I asked if I should write to Ann and Peter advised me to phone her.

Put the following into indirect speech:

1 'There's been an accident, and the road is blocked,' said the policeman. 'It won't be clear for some time. You'd better go round the other way.'

2 'Let's light a fire and cook our sausages over it,' said the children.

3 'I was thinking of going by bus,' said Paul.
'I shouldn't go by bus (if I were you),' said his aunt. 'It's an awfully bad service.'

4 'You'd better take sleeping bags; you may have to sleep out,' he warned us.

5 'I've left some books on your table,' said Peter. 'I think you'll find them useful. You can keep them as long as you need them but I'd like them back when you've finished with them.'
'Thank you very much,' I said. 'I'll take great care of them.'

6 'If children can learn a complicated language like Japanese by the time they are five,' said the Japanese professor, 'they should be able to learn the language of music. At the moment I'm teaching a class of forty three-year-olds to play the violin,' he added.

7 'The puppy can sleep on our bed,' said Tom.
'I'd rather he slept in a basket,' said his wife. 'That puppy will soon be a very big dog and then there won't be room for all three of us.'

8 'I'll try by myself first,' said Ann, 'and if I find that I can't manage, I'll ask Tom to help me.'

9 'Let's camp by this stream,' said Mary. 'If we go on, it may be dark before we find another good place.'

10 'I wish we'd brought our guitars,' said the students. 'Then we could have offered to play in the restaurant and perhaps they'd have given us a free meal.'

11 'I booked a double room on the first floor,' said Mr Jones.
'I'm afraid we didn't get your letter,' said the receptionist, 'and all the first and second floor rooms have been taken. But we could give you two single rooms on the third floor.'
'That wouldn't do me at all,' said Mr Jones.

12 'I've had gypsies on my land for two years,' said the farmer, 'and they've given nobody any trouble; but now the Council have asked me to tell them to move on. I don't see why they should be asked to move and I'm writing to my M.P. about it.'

13 'This letter is full of mistakes!' snorted Mr Jones.
'I did it in rather a hurry,' admitted the typist. 'I suppose I'd better type it again.'

14 'If you'd like to go on any of these tours,' said the receptionist, 'the hotel will arrange it.'
'We'd like to go on them all,' said the American couple.

15 'We'll try to find your passport,' said the policeman, 'but it'll be very difficult because a lot of suspicious characters sleep on the beach in summer and any one of them might have robbed you.'

16 'Let's go to the races!' said Ann. 'We might make our fortunes. I've been given a very good tip for the 2.30.'
'I've had "good tips" from you before,' said Paul. 'And they were disastrous.'

17 'I don't know why you waste so much time polishing the car,'
said Mr Jones.
'It preserves the paint,' said Mrs Jones, pausing for a moment.
'And besides, the neighbours all polish their cars and I don't
want our Mini to look like a poor relation. If you were any good,
you'd help me instead of standing there criticising,' she added.

18 'I'm sorry for not having a tie on,' said Peter. 'I didn't know it
was going to be a formal party.'

19 'I'd have enjoyed the journey more if the man in the berth below
mine hadn't snored all the time,' said Paul.

20 'I was thinking of going alone,' I said.
'You'd better take someone with you,' said the old man. 'It's
safer with two. One can keep watch while the other sleeps.'

21 (*Paul is speaking to Mary on the phone, and Mary is repeating his
words to Ann, who is standing beside her.*)
Paul: 'The plans have been changed. We're going tomorrow now,
not the next day. I want you to meet me at Victoria tonight to
arrange details.'
Mary: Paul says ...

22 'If I want a hot bath I have to put five pence in the meter,' said
Tom, 'and even then it's not very hot.'
'That's ridiculous,' I said; 'It's high time you left that place.'

23 'I know the umbrella belongs to you, but I thought it would be
all right if I borrowed it,' said my nephew, 'because you aren't
going out tomorrow and I am.'

24 'Let's put your tape-recorder under the table,' said Tom, 'and
make a recording of their conversation. It would be very useful
to know what they are planning.'
'But my recorder makes a distinct hum,' I said. 'They'd be sure
to hear it and look under the table; and then they'd find the
recorder and ask all sorts of embarrassing questions.'

25 'Whenever my father was unhappy,' said the girl, 'he would go
out and buy something, usually something large and useless.
That's why our rooms are full of things we can't use.'
'I'm sorry for your father,' said Tom, looking round. 'He must
have been a very unhappy man.'

26 'You can leave your motor cycle in my garage if you like,' he said.
'I'll keep an eye on it while you're away.'

27 'If you want a job you should read advertisements and write
letters and ring people up,' he said to Ann. 'It's no use sitting at
home, expecting employers to form a queue outside your door.'

28 'This used to be a lovely quiet street,' he said, 'but now it is impossible. When summer comes you'll have to keep the windows shut all the time because of the noise.'

29 'You must leave a note for your mother,' said Peter, 'otherwise she'll be terribly worried when you're not in at your usual time.'

30 'A telegram has just arrived for Albert,' said Mary, 'and he's on holiday. I wonder if I should ring him up and tell him about it or wait till he comes back.'

12 Reported Speech : Questions

[Sections 278, 279]

See note to exercise 10.
Put the following questions into indirect speech.

1 'Who has been using my typewriter?' said my mother.
2 'Do you want to see the cathedral?' said the guide.
3 'Do you mind working on the night shifts?' he asked.
4 'Would you like to come with us?' they said.
5 'Who did you give the money to?' asked Ann.
6 'How long does it take to get to Edinburgh by bus?' asked the tourist.
7 'How much do you think it will cost?' he said.
8 'What did you miss most when you were in prison?' Mary asked the ex-convict.
9 Another passenger came in and said, 'Is this seat taken?'
10 'How do you get on with your mother-in-law?' said Paul.
11 'How did you get into the house?' they asked him.
12 'What were you doing with these skeleton keys?' said Mr Jones. 'Were you trying to get at the secret files?'
13 'Did you sleep well?' asked my hostess.
14 'Have you been here long?' the other students asked him.
15 'Can you tell me why Paul left the university without taking his degree?' Paul's sister asked.
16 'How many people know the combination of the safe?' said the detective.
17 'Are there any letters for me?' said Mary.
18 'How long have you been learning English?' the examiner said.

19 'Why aren't you taking the exams?' said Paul.

20 'Are these free-range eggs?' said the customer.

21 'Where are you going for your summer holidays?' I asked them.

22 'Will it be all right if I come in a little later tonight?' asked the au pair girl.

23 'Would you mind if I shut the window?' said one of the passengers.

24 'Where can I park my caravan?' she asked the policeman.

25 'Would you like a lift?' said Ann.
'Which way are you going?' I said.

26 'Who do you want to speak to?' said the telephonist.

27 'Does anyone want tickets for the boxing match?' said Charles.

28 'What are you going to do with your old car?' I asked him.

29 'Do you grow your own vegetables?' I asked.

30 'What train are you going to get?' my friend inquired.

31 'Could you change a pound? I'm afraid I haven't got anything smaller,' said the passenger to the conductor.

32 'How many sleeping pills have you taken?' said the night sister.
'I have no idea,' said Mr Jones sleepily.

33 'Could we see the manager, please?' said the two men.
'Have you an appointment?' said the secretary.

34 'Do you think you could live entirely on your own for six months' said Tom, 'or would you get bored?'

35 'Did any of you actually see the accident happen?' said the policeman.

36 'Could I see Commander Smith?' the lady asked.
'I'm afraid he's in orbit,' I said. 'Would you like to leave a message?'

13 Reported Speech: Questions, Advice, Requests, Invitations, Suggestions

[Sections 278, 279, 282, 287]

(i) **'What about'** often introduces a suggestion and is then reported by **suggest**:

'What about flying?' he said. He suggested flying.

'I can't come at 1.0,' said Ann. 'Then what about 2.0?' said Tom. Ann said she couldn't come at 1.0, so Tom suggested 2.0.

(ii) **'Why don't you'** often introduces suggestions or advice and is then reported by **suggest** or **advise**:

'I wonder if Tom is coming,' said Ann. 'Why don't you ask him?' I said.

Ann wondered if Tom was coming. I advised her to ask him, or: I suggested (her) asking him.

(iii) **'Could I have'** is normally reported by **ask for**:

'Could I have a cup of coffee?' she said.

She asked (me) for a cup of coffee.

'Could you' used for requests is reported by **ask**:

'Could you sign the book, please?' he said.

He asked me to sign the book.

But when **'Could you'** introduces an ordinary question the verb is reported unchanged:

'Could you live entirely on your own?' he said.

He asked if I could live entirely on my own.

(iv) **'Would you mind waiting/signing'** etc. can be reported:

He asked me to wait/sign etc., or:

He asked if I would mind waiting/signing etc.

(v) **Offer** can be used in two constructions:

'Would you like a drink?'

He offered me a drink.

'Shall I wait for you/I'll wait for you if you like.'

He offered to wait for me.

When the infinitive is used it must be placed *directly after* **offer**. The person addressed is not mentioned in this construction.

Put the following into indirect speech.

1 'Shall we have dinner somewhere after the theatre?' said Peter. 'Yes, let's,' said Ann. 'What about going to that place Jack is always talking about?' (*for* **Yes, let's** *put*: Ann agreed)

2 'Jack's parents have asked me to supper tomorrow night,' said Ann. 'What shall I wear?'

'I should wear something warm, dear,' said her mother. 'It's a terribly cold house.'

3 'I'm broke,' said Jack.
'Shall I lend you some money?' said Peter.

4 'It will take a little time to look up your file,' said the clerk.
'Is it worth waiting?' said Ann, 'or shall I go away and come back later?'

5 'Shall I have to do the whole exam again if I fail in one paper?' said the student.
'Yes,' said the teacher.

6 'Where will you be tomorrow,' I said, 'in case I have to ring you?'
'I shall be in my office till six,' said the old man, 'and after that at my flat. I shan't be going to the club.'

7 'What shall I do with this cracked cup?' Mary asked.
'You'd better throw it away,' said her mother.

8 'Shall I ever see him again?' she wondered.

9 'Would you mind getting out of the car?' said the driver. 'I have to change a wheel.'
'Shall I help you?' I said.

10 'I've run out of petrol,' said the man. 'Could you possibly give me a lift to the next village?'

11 'Shall we go for a walk?' said Peter.
'I like walking,' said Ann, 'but at the moment my only comfortable walking shoes are being mended. What about going for a drive instead?'

12 'You've got a lot of parcels,' he said. 'Shall I carry some of them for you?'

13 'Shall we be in time?' muttered Tom, looking at his watch.
(use **wonder**)

14 'What shall I do with all this foreign money?' said Peter.
'Why don't you take it to the bank and get it changed?' said Mary.

15 'Would you like a cigarette?' said Peter.
'No, thanks,' said Jack. 'I don't smoke.'

16 'Would you like to come with us?' they said. 'There's plenty of room in the car.'
'I'd love to,' said Ann.

17 (*Telephone conversation*):
Ann: Could you do without me today, Mr Jones? I've got an awful cold and I think it might be better if I stayed at home.
Mr Jones: I should certainly stay at home, Ann. And you'd better take tomorrow off too if you aren't better.

18 Mary (on phone): Paul, I've just come back to my flat to find a complete stranger asleep in my chair. He's still here, and still asleep! What shall I do?
Paul: Why don't you wake him up and ask him who he is? There's probably some quite simple explanation.

19 'I'm not quite ready,' said Peter. 'Could you wait a few minutes?'
'I can't wait long,' said Jack. 'The train goes at ten.'

20 'Would you mind taking off your hat?' I said to the woman in front of me.
'But the theatre's almost empty!' she said. 'Why don't you move along a bit?'

21 'I often see lights in the empty house across the road,' said Albert. 'Do you think I should report it?'

22 'If this house was yours what changes would you make?' I said.
'I'd pull it down and build a modern one on the same site,' said the window-cleaner. 'The site's all right.'

23 'Could I have your name and address, please?' said the travel agent.

24 'Shall I send it round to your hotel, sir?' the shop assistant asked the tourist.
'I'm not staying in the town,' said the tourist. 'I'll take it with me.'

25 'How long will you go on looking for them?' I asked one of the search party.
'We'll go on till we find them,' he said. 'But we don't search at night. We'll stop when it gets dark and start again at first light tomorrow.'

26 'We can't discuss this over the phone. We'd better meet,' I said.
'Shall we meet here in my flat tomorrow?'
'I'd rather you came to my office,' he said. 'Could you get here in half an hour?'

27 'Could I have five pence, please?' said the boy. 'I want to buy an ice-cream.'

28 'Would you like to sleep on the floor of my flat?' he asked us.
'Or would you rather go to a hotel?'

29 'Could you help me with my luggage, please?' she said. 'If you take the two big ones I'll take the small one.'
'It's ridiculous to take three suitcases for a weekend,' I said. 'Couldn't you manage with two?'
'No,' she said.

30 'I couldn't come on Monday,' said Ann.
'Then what about Tuesday,' said Peter.
'All right,' said Ann.

14 Reported Speech: Commands, Requests, Invitations, Advice

[Sections 280, 281, 287]

Put the following sentences into indirect speech, using **tell/
order/urge/ask/beg/invite/advise/warn/remind**
+ object + infinitive, or **ask** (+ object) + **for**, or, in some
cases, **ask** + infinitive.

1 'Don't put sticky things in your pockets,' said his mother.
2 'Please, please don't do anything dangerous,' said his wife.
3 'Go on—apply for the job,' said my friend. 'It would just suit you.'
4 'I should say nothing about it (if I were you),' said my brother.
5 'Would you please wait in the lounge till your flight number is
called?' she said.
6 'Don't lend Harry any money,' I said to Ann. 'He never pays his
debts.'
7 'Could you please ring back in half an hour?' said the secretary.
8 'Would you mind moving your case?' said the other passenger.
'It's blocking the door.'
9 'Remember to book a table,' said Ann.
10 'Get into the right lane,' said the driving instructor.
11 'Avoid Marble Arch,' said the policeman. 'There's going to be a
big demonstration there.'
12 'Hold the ladder,' he said. 'It's rather unsteady.'
'Why don't you tie it at the top?' I said. 'It's much safer that way.'
13 'Read the questions twice,' said the teacher, 'and don't write in
the margin.'
14 'You'd better not leave your money lying about,' said one of the
students.
15 'Why don't you open a bank account?' said another. (*use* **advise**)
16 'Would you like to have lunch with me today?' said the tourist.

'I'd love to but I'm afraid I can't leave the office,' said the girl.

17 'Don't take more than two of these at once,' said the doctor, handing me a bottle of pills.

18 'Could I speak to Albert, please?' I said.
'He's still asleep,' said his mother.
'Then please wake him,' I said. 'I have news for him.'

19 'I'd buy the big tin if I were you,' said the grocer.

20 'You're being exploited,' said the other au pair girls. 'You ought to leave your job.'

21 'Fasten your seat belts, there may be a little turbulence,' said the air hostess.

22 'Don't drive through fog with only a fog light on,' he said, 'or oncoming drivers may take you for a motor cycle.'

23 'Could I see your driving licence?' said the policeman.

24 'You'd better sweep up that broken glass,' I said.

25 'The bathroom's empty now,' she said. 'Will you put the light out when you've finished?'

26 'Remember to insure your luggage,' my father said.

27 'Please don't drink any more,' said his wife. 'Don't forget that we have to drive home.'

28 'Do go to a dentist, Tom, before your toothache gets any worse,' I said.

29 'Why don't you cut your hair?' he said. 'You'd find it much easier to get a job with short hair.'

30 'Could I have some more pudding, please?' said the boy.

15 Reported Speech: Commands, Requests, Advice, Suggestions

[Sections 280–282, 287

Read notes to previous exercises.
Put the following into indirect speech, using either the constructions recommended in Exercise 14, or: **suggest** or: **say** + subject + **is to/are to/was to/were to** or: **should**

1 'Would you please fill up this form and then join the queue by the door?' said the clerk.

2 'Could you read the last sentence again, please?' said the examiner.

3 'Could I have a new cheque book, please?' said the girl.
'Could you show me your old cheque book?' said the bank clerk.

4 Telegram: Be ready to move off at very short notice. Tom.
Ann (reading it to Mary): Tom says that we .... .

5 'Please, please don't tell my mother,' begged the boy.

6 'Don't fire except in self-defence,' said the police sergeant.

7 'Why don't you take the rest of the day off?' said my assistant.

8 'Will you help me to move the piano, please?' said my aunt.

9 'Don't drive too close to the car in front,' said the driving instructor.

10 'Don't smoke near the petrol pump,' said the mechanic.

11 'When you've chosen a book, bring it to me and I'll stamp it,' said the librarian.

12 'Show the boarding card to the man at the foot of the gangway,' said the clerk.

13 'Reduce speed now,' said a huge notice. (*omit* **now**)

14 'Could I see your ticket, please?' said the inspector.

15 'Keep an eye on your luggage,' he said. 'This place is full of thieves.'

16 'When you have read this, pass it on to the next person on the list,' he said.

17 'Will you stand still!' he said angrily.

18 'Whenever you see the number "7" on the screen, press this button,' he said.

19 'Sit down and tell me what is worrying you,' he said to her.

20 'Walk along the line of men,' said the police sergeant, 'and if you recognise your attacker, just nod. Don't say anything.'

21 'Even if you feel hungry don't eat anything between meals,' said the dietician.

22 'Could you ring up the taxi rank and order a taxi for me?' said Tom.
'Why don't you go by tube?' said Ann. 'It's much quicker.'

23 'Let's buy some yeast and make our own bread,' said Mary.
'The bread we're getting now is absolutely tasteless.'

24 'If you have to use the river water,' said the guide, 'boil it first. Don't drink it unboiled.'

25 'Let's not tell anyone,' said Tom, 'till we are quite certain that the report is true.'

26 Tom (*on phone to Ann*): I've got the tickets. Meet me at the air terminal at 6.30.

(Imagine that you are Ann. Report this message to Mary, who is standing beside you. Begin: Tom says . . .)

27 'Let us show that we are united,' urged the strike leader, 'by voting unanimously to continue the strike. Let every man put his hand up when the vote is taken!'

28 'Will customers please count their change,' said a notice above the cashier's desk, 'as mistakes cannot be rectified afterwards.'

29 'Don't clap yet,' warned my friend. 'She hasn't finished. Singers loathe people who clap too soon,' he added.

30 'Don't forget to put your name at the top of the page,' said the supervisor.

16 Reported Speech: Mixed   [Chapter 28]

(i) Read the notes to previous reported speech exercises.

(ii) Note that **want** or **would like** is often useful when the speaker reports a request made to himself or made through him to someone else:

Tom *(on phone to Ann)*: Could you book me a room in a hotel for tonight?

Ann *(telling Mary about this)*: Tom wants me to book him a room for tonight.

Tom says that I am to book *would also be possible but more authoritative.*

Similarly:

Mrs Jones *(on the phone to Mary)*: Could you ask Mrs Smith to ring me back?

Mary *(telling Mrs Smith about it)*: Mrs Jones rang. She

| wants | you to ring her back. |
| would like | |

She says that you are to ring *would be possible but very authoritative.*

1 *(Letter from Paul to Ann)*: Please get me a small tent and camping equipment for two people.

Ann *(telling Mary about this)*: Paul wants . . .

2 Mr White *(on phone to Mr Black's secretary)*: Ask Mr Black to meet me at six in the bar on the ground floor.

Secretary *(reporting this to Mr Black)*: Mr White would like . . .

3 'Shall I go and get a candle?' said Ann when the light went out suddenly.
'I'd rather you got another bulb,' said Mr Jones.
'But there aren't any,' said Ann, 'and the shops are shut.'

4 'Don't worry about a few mistakes,' said Peter. 'I make mistakes all the time.'
'Do you learn from your mistakes?' I asked. 'Or do you keep making the same ones?'

5 'I'm looking for a man called Albert, who drinks in this bar. Could you point him out to me when he comes in?' I said.
'I should keep away from Albert if I were you,' said the barman. 'He doesn't like strangers and might turn nasty.'

6 'Could I have a look at your paper for a moment?' said the man next to me. 'I just want to see the football results.'
'I haven't quite finished with it,' I said. 'Could you wait a moment?'
'I can't wait long,' he said. 'I'm getting off at the next stop.'

7 'You woke everyone up last night,' said my mother. 'You must try to be quieter tonight.'
'We will,' I promised.

8 'The soup's cold again,' complained Mr Jones. 'Why do I never have hot soup?'
'Because the kitchen's half a mile from the dining room,' explained his wife. 'If you insist on living in a castle you must put up with its disadvantages.'
'What about getting an au pair girl, an ex-Olympic runner?' said Mr Jones.
'She wouldn't stay,' sighed his wife.

9 'Your licence is out of date,' said the policeman.
'It is,' I admitted, 'but I've applied for a new one.'
'Next time,' he said severely, 'apply for a new one before your present one has expired.'

10 'I'll have the money for you next week. Shall I post it to you?' I said.
'Could you keep it in your safe till I can come and collect it?' said Tom. 'A lot of my mail has been going astray lately and I'd hate to lose one of your large cheques.'

11 'Could I borrow your map again?' said Peter.
'You're always borrowing it. Why don't you get one of your own?' I said.

12 'When you hear the fire bell,' he said, 'shut the windows and go downstairs.'

'And what shall we do if the stairs are blazing?' I asked.

13 'Do you hear that noise?' Ann said. 'What do you think it is?'
'I think it's only rats running up and down inside the wall,' I said.
'I think it's someone trying to get in,' she said, 'You'd better go and see.'

14 It's your turn to baby-sit tonight,' they told Ann.
'It can't be!' said Ann indignantly. 'I baby-sat last night! And the night before! And I'm only supposed to do two nights a week!'
'Could you possibly do it just this once?' they said. 'And we promise not to ask you to do any next week.'

15 'This is the best restaurant in town,' said the taxi driver. 'The only problem is that they expect guests to wear ties.'
'Then why have you brought us here?' said the tourists indignantly.
'Don't get excited,' said the taxi-driver, opening a box. 'I keep ties specially for gentlemen in your predicament. What colour would you like? They're all the same price.'

16 'Shall I start tomorrow?' I said.
'I'd rather you started today,' said Tom.

17 'Why don't you go and see the film? It may help you to understand the book,' I said.
'But the film's quite different from the book,' Ann pointed out.

18 'I saw the two climbers,' said the helicopter pilot. 'And one of them sat up and waved to me.'
'Which of them waved?' I said.
'I don't know,' he answered. 'I wasn't near enough to see them clearly.'

19 'What caused the ship to sink?' I said.
'She must have struck the submerged wreck,' said the coxswain of the lifeboat. 'But I can't understand it, because the wreck is very clearly marked with buoys.'

20 'My car won't start!' exclaimed Mary. 'The battery's flat again! Could you possibly give me a push just to start me down the hill?'
'Why don't you sell that car?' said Bill.
'Nobody would buy it,' said Peter. 'What about just putting a match to it?'
'We'll give you a little push,' said Jack, standing up. 'But check that there's petrol in it first, and remember to switch on.'

21 'I've been given so many bottles of wine lately that I'll have to buy another wine rack,' said Mr Jones.
'Why don't you throw a party and save yourself the expense of a wine rack?' I suggested.

22 'Press Button A to start the engine,' he said.
'But last time you told me to press button B!' I said.
'That was on a slightly different type of machine,' he explained.

23 'Don't brake if you find yourself skidding,' said Tom. 'That only makes it worse. Try to steer into the skid.'
'I know what I *should* do,' I said. 'But when I start skidding I get so excited that I do the exact opposite.'
'Then stop and let me take over,' said Tom. 'We're just coming to an icy bit and I don't want to die just yet.'

24 'I've run out of stamps,' said my father. 'Have you got any?'
'No, but I'll go out and get you some if you like,' I said.
'Don't bother,' he said. 'I've missed the post anyway.'

25 'Repairs to cars rented from us must be arranged through our office,' he said. 'So if anything goes wrong with the one you've hired, please ring the number printed on your card. The office is open from nine to six, Monday to Friday.'
'But what shall I do if something goes wrong with it outside office hours?' I said.

26 'Why didn't you signal to the tanker that she was coming too close?' I said.
'We did signal,' said the pilot, 'but she came on in and ran aground.'
'What's going to happen to her?' I said.
'We're going to try to tow her off at the next high tide,' he said. 'But if we don't get her off tonight she'll be here till she breaks up, and there'll be an oil slick all along the coast.'

27 'Why are you spending so long on those accounts?' I asked.
'Because I can't make them balance,' he said. 'I seem to be £13 short; and that means that I'll have to put in £13 of my own money to make it up.'
'Would you like me to go through them and see if I can find a mistake?' I said.
'No,' he said, 'but I'd like you to lend me £13.'

28 'Why are you looking so depressed, Jack?' I said.
'Because I've just asked Ann to marry me and she's refused,' he said sadly.
'I think she prefers clean-shaven men,' I said. 'Why don't you cut your hair and shave off your beard and try again?'

29 'How did you get up that tree?' Mary asked.
'I used a ladder, of course,' he snapped. 'But someone went off with it when I was sawing. Go and get another one and don't just stand there asking silly questions.'

30 'Are you ill?' he said coldly.
'No,' I said.
'Did you sleep well last night?'
'Yes,' I said.
'Then why are you sitting about when all the others are working? Go out at once and give them a hand.'

31 'Will passengers with nothing to declare please go through the green door?' said a customs official.
'You'd better go through the green door, Mary,' said Peter, 'but I'll have to go through the other one. I'll take a bit longer than you will, so wait for me at the other end.'

32 (*Imagine that you have received the following post card from your brother, Tom. Report it at once to the other members of the family. Begin:* Tom says ...)
Don't worry about me. I wasn't badly injured and I'm being very well looked after. I'm coming back next Wednesday on the nine o'clock flight from Zurich. Could you please meet the plane?

33 'What shall I do with my wet shoes?' said the boy.
'You'd better put newspaper in them and put them near the fire,' said his mother. 'But don't put them too near or they'll go hard.'

34 'Let's drive on to the next village and try the hotel there,' he said.
'But what'll we do if that's full too?' I asked.
'We'll just have to sleep in the car,' he said. 'It will be too late to try anywhere else.'

35 'They have a rather fierce dog,' said Ann; 'but he's a heavy sleeper, and with any luck won't hear you breaking in.'
'What'll I do if he wakes up?' I said.
'If he starts growling, give him some of these biscuits,' said Ann.
'How do you know that he likes these particular biscuits?'
'All dogs like them,' Ann assured me. 'It says so on the packet.'

36 'If you even touch one of the pictures,' warned the attendant, 'alarm bells will ring all over the gallery and you will be arrested instantly.'
'Are you serious?' I said.
'Try it and see,' he answered with a glint in his eye.

EXERCISES

Exercise 1

1. are you going,we'll probably go 2. are having,is leaving/leaves 3. shall/will see,will probably look 4. am seeing,will refuse 5. shall/will know,will tell 6. will be,shall/will miss,will/shall walk,will probably catch 7. shall/will probably come,will give,am coming 8. will get,are staying,will have to,will/ shall move 9. will he say,won't mind,will just buy 10. won't know,will/ shall leave 11. will never get,will meet,will fall 12. am going,are you coming, shall/will probably have 13. are you walking,will get,will bring 14. am having, are starting,will make 15. are you taking,am taking,will pass,will/shall take 16. are you meeting,are meeting,is taking 17. are you doing,will/shall go,will/ shall probably stay 18. is Jack arriving,is he getting,will come 19. are they doing,are going,is happening,are taking,will enjoy 20. will wake,won't get 21. are spending,shall/will manage,will turn,will be able 22. is catching,will be 23. is George coming,are moving,shall/will have to 24. am ringing,shall I ask,shall/will be,will/shall write 25. are having,are lunching,is standing,are giving 26. will let,shall/will find 27. are getting,are you going,are they having 28. shall I wait,will take 29. will you have,will have,will have,are having,am having,will have 30. will give,am collecting 31. is getting,will happen,will ring,will sleep,will come 32. am being,is leaving,am taking, will soon be,will spend,will lose (or: will spend . . . and lose) 33. am flying,are you taking, will spend 34. are going,are having . . . and going, will come,is coming,will/ shall ask 35. is coming,shall we go,will/shall get,shall/will be able, won't/ shan't pay 36. are opening,are having,will look,will come,are you having,are missing,are going

Exercise 2

1. are you going,am going,are you going to do,am going to fish 2. are you going,am not going,am staying/going to stay,am going to write 3. is going to rain 4. are you staying,am going,are you going to do,am going to try 5. am going to dye,are you going to do,are you going to have it done,am going to read 6. am going to read 7. are you doing,are coming, am going to show/am showing,are you taking,am going to take/am taking 8. are starting,are going,are you going to climb,is going to climb,am going to sit . . . and do 9. are going,are you going to feed,are taking/are going to take,are going to try 10. aren't you going to ask,am leaving,are you going to do,are you going to have,am going to start 11. are you going to use,am going to live,am going to start,are you going to do/are you doing,am selling/am going to sell,is getting 12. is going,is having,is going to look,is coming 13. am going to send,am seeing 14. is arriving,is he spending,is he catching,is spending,is giving . . . and attending 15. is he bringing,is going to do,is giving 16. am starting,are you going to do,am going to study 17. are you going, am going to get,am going, am going to ask,is joining/is going to join,they are all going to pick 18. am going to buy,is going to be 19. are you going to do,are you going to sell,am going to learn,am having 20. am moving in,are you going to have,am going to paint 21. are you having,am going to do/am doing,am going to use, are going to help,am hiring/am going to hire 22. am going to do,am going to plant . . . and make,are you going to give/are you giving 23. am getting,are starting,is coming 24. are meeting,are they just going to repeat,are they going to climb,are going to offer

Exercise 3

1. am going to have 2. are going to assemble,will come 3. am going to shampoo 4. am going to make,will burn 5. am going to paint 6. am going to make 7. will look 8. will see 9. will wait 10. are going to camp . . . and cook 11. am going to put 12. are you going to wear,am going to sit . . . and watch, am not going to get 13. will take 14. will have 15. will start,will get,will bake 16. is going to bake,will soon get 17. are you going to try,am going to try,

will confiscate 18. shall/will have,will come 19. am not going to take,am going to mend,is going to help 20. are you going to paint,am going to take 21. will add,won't be able to read,am going to type,shall/will have 22. will type 23. will ring 24. am going to ring 25. aren't you going to climb,are going to climb,are going to try,will cook,will buy 26. am going to wash,will come 27. are going to pick,will probably come,will all start 28. will have to go,will be,will get,will you let 29. will stay,will try 30. am going to start, are you going to do,is going to help 31. is going to write,will buy,will buy 32. is going to dig 33. is going to make,is going to concentrate 34. are going to bottle 35. will go 36. are going to buy,will stay

Exercise 4

1. shall/will both be coming 2. will meet,will forget 3. will be cooking,will/ shall ring 4. shall/will be doing,will still be working 5. will get,will do 6. will be coming 7. shall/will be working 8. shall/will be taking off 9. will come 10. will be playing 11. will get,will still be,will be going,will ask 12. will be, will be wondering/will wonder 13. shall/will never be able,will be helping, won't be helping,will be helping 14. will write,will try,will type 15. shall/ will be typing,will type 16. will tell 17. will just be coming 18. will be melting 19. will be talking . . . and showing,shall/will feel 20. will/shall tell, won't believe 21. will just be getting up 22. will be wearing,will wrap . . . and go 23. will be,will be speaking,will be addressing 24. will be reading,will be ringing 25. will still be standing 26. will you please forward,shall/will be staying 27. will be coming 28. will be leaving 29. won't start,will give 30. will be coming 31. will be looking 32. will you be arriving,shall/will be travelling,will there be,will send 33. will you be using,will put 34. shall/will be having,will be lying 35. will enjoy,shan't/won't have,shall/will be mapreading,shall/will be 36. will write

Exercise 5

1. won't do 2. won't come,won't be driving 3. shan't/won't be coming 4. won't have,won't come 5. shan't/won't be teaching 6. shall/will be doing, shan't/won't be eating 7. won't eat 8. won't bite 9. won't be coming 10. will be fishing 11. won't clean 12. shan't/won't be showing 13. shan't/won't be washing,shall/will be having 14. shan't/won't be wearing,won't recognise 15. won't be,won't believe 16. shan't/won't be delivering 17. won't be wearing 18. won't tell 19. won't be using,won't do 20. shall/will have,shan't/won't be paying 21. won't pay,will have 22. won't work 23. will get on/won't be working 24. won't even show,won't come

Exercise 6

shall used here is replaceable by will

1. will have repaired 2. will have done 3. shall have made 4. will have finished 5. will have planted 6. shall have passed 7. shall have done 8. will have walked 9. will have lost 10. will have spent 11. shall have worked 12. will have been driven 13. shall have sent 14. shall have given 15. will have died 16. will have driven 17. shall have picked 18. will have sunk

Exercise 7

(shall is not replaceable by will)

1. shall,will 2. will 3. shall,will 4. will 5. will 6. shan't,shan't,will,shall 7. will 8. shall 9. will,won't 10. will 11. shall,shall,won't 12. will 13. shan't 14. won't 15. shall,shall not 16. will,shall 17. shall,will,will,won't 18. shall, will 19. shan't,will 20. shall,will 21. shan't,will 22. Will,won't 23. shan't,will 24. shall

Exercise 8

1. begins 2. gets 3. open 4. are 5. start 6. receive/have received 7. like 8. are 9. slows 10. stops 11. will/shall explain,are 12. read/have read 13. have been 14. have cleaned ... and painted/clean ... and paint 15. have settled/settle 16. see 17. have seen 18. have finished/finish 19. have reached/reach 20. have done 21. lifts/has lifted 22. arrives 23. know,will give 24. has cooled/cools 25. have finished/finish 26. have given 27. will tell,get 28. have been,will let 29. have flown 30. has been 31. come 32. shall/will have finished,see,finish/have finished,start 33. have seen 34. have driven 35. will/shall give,wakes 36. arrived

Exercise 9

1. gets 2. come 3. stops 4. have done 5. saw 6. comes 7. go/are going 8. get, see 9. come,cross 10. arrive,gets 11. am sitting,am walking 12. has finished/finishes 13. starts 14. have paid/pay 15. arrives 16. have worked 17. do/are doing 18. have done 19. have eaten 20. have had 21. have been 22. have read 23. reached 24. has saved 25. are queueing 26. shall/will be cruising 27. am 28. have seen 29. retires/has retired 30. has saved 31. stopped 32. arrived 33. had finished/finished 34. am waiting 35. was cleaning or pretending 36. needed

Exercise 10

1. he said he was going out but he'd be in 2. she said she was working and didn't much care 3. Peter said he couldn't live on his basic salary and he'd have to 4. Mary said her young brother wanted to be ... she couldn't think why because none of her family had ever been 5. they said they were waiting ... and it was late 6. he said he had made ... I said he was always making ... and should be used to it 7. he said they made ... and sent ... to their wives 8. he said it was lonely being away from their ... but they earned ... in that/the factory as they would in their own 9. he said they had been there ... and were going to stay 10. he said he'd got ... I said that would be ... he replied he knew it would be hard but he didn't mind ... and it would be 11. he said the ice would soon be ... she said she would look for her skates when she got 12. she said she was living with her parents at the moment but she hoped to have a flat of her own shortly 13. she said she was leaving the following day ... we said we'd come and see her off 14. he said he'd just bought ... but it wasn't insured yet so he couldn't take me 15. she said she would like to come ... but she was bathing ... and they would drown if she left 16. Ann says she is coming ... next week. She hopes we will meet her ... 17. She said nothing ever happened ... it was like ... people had gone 18. he said he had missed his train; he'd be late ... and his boss would be 19. they said they would wait for me if I was late/for us if we were late 20. I said they were supposed ... but if the fog got ... the plane might be 21. she said if I lent she'd bring ... in two days' time 22. he grumbled he hated getting up on dark mornings; his wife agreed it was horrible but said the mornings would be lighter soon and then it wouldn't be 23. she said the sales were starting the following day and as soon as they finished work the whole ... pool was going ... I (said I) hoped they would all get what they wanted 24. he (said he) wished he had something ... said he had only just had lunch and she didn't know how he could be ... 25. my aunt said if I was short ... she could lend me ... and I could take my time 26. he said he usually took his dog ... when he came ... 27. I said I had a ... for her brother. Ann said he wasn't at home; he had left two days before 28. I said I had bought the hat ... he said I shouldn't have bought ... it didn't go with my coat 29. she said she must hurry as her father was always ...if any of them were 30. he said if I wanted to smoke I would have to 31. he said he was building himself ...

he wouldn't show it to me just yet but when the roof was on I could come 32. he said the lake would probably freeze that night; it was much colder than the previous night. Mary said she would go . . . and if it was frozen she would make . . . ducks could 33. He said . . . the strikers went back the following day it would be . . . things returned 34. She said someone was trying to murder her, she kept getting 35. she said she was taking her children . . . the following day 36. she said all she could hear was . . . she wondered if it was . . .

Exercise 11

1. he said there had been . . . road was blocked . . . it wouldn't be clear . . . he advised us to/he said we'd better go 2. they suggested lighting . . . cooking their sausages 3. he said he was thinking . . . aunt advised him not to go . . . as it was a bad 4. she warned us to take . . . as we might have to 5. he said he had left some books on my table. He thought I'd find them useful and said I could keep them as long as I needed them but that he'd like . . . when I had finished with them. I thanked him and said I'd take/promised to take . . . 6. he said that if children could . . . were . . . should be able . . . he was teaching 7. he said the puppy could sleep on their bed . . . she said she'd rather he slept . . . would soon be . . . there wouldn't be . . . all three of them 8. she said she'd try by herself . . . and if she found that she couldn't . . . she'd ask 9. Mary suggested camping by the stream as, (*or:* pointing out that) if they went on, it might be dark before they found 10. they wished they'd brought their . . . as then they could have offered . . . and perhaps they (the restaurant) would have given them 11. Jones said he'd booked . . . . The receptionist said she (was afraid that they) hadn't got . . . all rooms had been taken . . . but they could give him . . . Jones said that wouldn't do him 12. he said he'd had gypsies on his land and they'd given . . . Council had asked him . . . . He didn't see why . . . and was writing to his M.P. 13. he grumbled that the letter was . . . . She admitted she had done it . . . and said she supposed she'd better 14. he said if they'd like to go on any of the tours the hotel would arrange it. They said they'd like 15. he said they'd try to find my passport but it would be . . . slept . . . might have robbed me 16. she suggested going . . . and said they might make their . . . . She'd been given . . . . He said he had had . . . from her . . . they had been 17. he said he didn't know why she wasted . . . she said it preserved . . . all polished . . . she didn't want their Mini . . . . If he were any good . . . he'd help her 18. he apologised for not having a tie on. He said he didn't know it was going 19. he said he would have enjoyed . . . the berth below his hadn't snored 20. I said I was thinking . . . he advised me to take someone with me. It was safer as one could . . . slept 21. Paul says that the plans have been changed; we're going tomorrow now not the next day. He wants us to meet him at Victoria tonight 22. He said that if he wanted . . . he had to . . . it wasn't hot. I said that was ridiculous and that it was high time he left 23. he said he knew the umbrella belonged to me but he thought it would be all right if he borrowed it because I wasn't going out the following day and he was 24. he suggested putting my . . . and making . . . It would be . . . what they were planning. I said/ objected that my recorder made . . . and they'd be sure . . . and then they'd find . . . and ask 25. she said whenever her father was unhappy he would go out and buy . . . their rooms were full . . . they couldn't use. Tom said that he was sorry for her father; he must have been 26. he said I could leave my . . . in his garage if I liked . . . he would keep . . . while I was away 27. he told Ann that if she wanted a job she should read . . . it was no use . . . outside her door 28. he said it used to be . . . but that now it was impossible. When summer came I'd have to 29. he said I must leave a note for my . . . otherwise she'd be . . . when I wasn't in at my 30. she said

. . . had just arrived . . . and he was . . . She wondered if she should ring
. . . wait till he came

Exercise 12

1. she asked who had been using her 2. he asked if I wanted 3. he asked if I
minded 4. they asked if I would like to come with them/they invited me to
come with them 5. she asked who I had given 6. he asked how long it took
7. he asked how much I thought it would cost 8. she asked him what he had
missed most when he was/had been 9. he asked if the seat was taken 10. He
asked how I got on with my 11. they asked him how he had got 12. he asked
what I was/had been doing with the skeleton . . . and if I was/had been
trying 13. she asked me if I had slept 14. they asked him if he had been
there 15. she asked if I could tell her why Paul (had) left 16. he asked how
many . . . knew 17. she asked if there were . . . for her 18. he asked how
long I had been 19. he asked why I wasn't 20. the customer asked if they
were 21. I asked where they were going for their 22. she asked if it would be
. . . if she came . . . that night 23. he asked if I would mind if he shut
24. she asked him where she could park her 25. she asked if I would like
. . . I asked which way she was going 26. she asked who I wanted. 27. he
asked if anyone wanted 28. I asked what he was going to do with his 29. I
asked if she grew her own 30. he asked what train I was going 31. she asked
him if he could change . . . and said she was afraid she hadn't got/and
apologised for not having 32. she asked how many . . . he had taken. He
said he had no idea 33. they asked if they could see the manager/they asked
to see the manager. The secretary asked if they had 34. he asked if I thought
I could live . . . on my own . . . or if I would get 35. he asked if any of us
had actually seen 36. she asked if she could see/she asked to see/she asked
for Commander Smith. I said I was afraid he was in orbit and asked if she
would like

Exercise 13

1. he suggested having . . . Ann agreed and suggested going . . . Jack was
always 2. she said Jack's parents had asked her . . . the following night and
asked what she should wear. Her mother advised her to wear . . . as it was a
3. he said he was broke. Peter offered to lend him 4. the clerk said it would
take . . . to look up her file. Ann asked if it was worth waiting or if she
should 5. he asked if he would have to do . . . if he failed . . . The teacher
said that he would 6. I asked where he would be the next day in case I had
to ring him. He said that he would be in his . . . at his flat. He wouldn't be
going 7. Mary asked what she should do with the cracked cup and her mother
advised her to throw 8. she wondered if she would ever see 9. he asked me
to get out . . . as he had to change . . . I offered to help 10. he said he'd
run . . . and asked me to give him/asked for a lift 11. he suggested going
. . . She said she liked . . . but that her only . . . shoes were being . . . She
suggested going 12. he said I had a lot . . . and offered to carry some of
them for me 13. she wondered if they would be 14. he asked what he should
do with all the money. Mary advised him to take . . . and get/Mary
suggested taking . . . and getting 15. Peter offered Jack a cigarette. Jack
thanked him and said he didn't smoke 16. They asked if she'd like to
go/invited her to go with them, saying that there was . . . Ann said she'd
love to/Ann accepted 17. she asked Mr Jones if he could do without her
that day as she had . . . and thought it might . . . if she stayed. Mr Jones
advised her to stay . . . and to take the next day off too if she wasn't better.
18. Mary told Paul she'd just come back to her flat . . . in her chair.
He was still there . . . and she asked/wanted to know what she should do.
Paul advised her to wake him and ask him who he was, adding that there was
19. he said he wasn't quite . . . and asked Jack to wait/if he could wait . . .

Jack said he couldn't wait long because the train went . . . 20. I asked her to take off her hat/if she would mind taking . . . She pointed out that the theatre was . . . and suggested my/me moving 21. he said he often saw . . . and asked if I thought he should . . . 22. I asked what changes he would make if the house was his. He said he'd pull . . . The site was all right 23. he asked for my name 24. he offered to send it round to his hotel/asked if he should send . . . The tourist said he wasn't staying . . . and he'd take it with him 25. I asked (him) how long they would go on looking . . . He said they'd go on till they found them. But they didn't search . . . they'd stop when it got . . . and start . . . the following day 26. I said we couldn't discuss it over the phone . . . and suggested meeting in my flat the following day. He said he'd rather I came to his . . . and asked if I could get there 27. he asked for five pence to buy an ice-cream/as he wanted to buy an ice-cream 28. he asked (us) if we would like . . . of his flat, or if we would rather . . . 29. she asked me to help her with her luggage, and said that if I took . . . she'd take . . . I said it was ridiculous . . . and asked if she couldn't manage . . . but she said she couldn't 30. Ann said she couldn't come . . . (so) Peter suggested Tuesday . . . Ann agreed (to this)

Exercise 14

(The verb of command given below is not necessarily the only possible one
1. she told him not to put . . . in his 2. she begged him not to do 3. he urged me to apply . . . as it would just suit me 4. he advised me to say nothing 5. she asked them to wait in the lounge till their flight number was called 6. I advised her not to lend . . . as he never paid 7. she asked him to ring 8. he asked me to move my case/asked if I'd mind moving my case as it was blocking 9. she reminded him to book 10. he told/warned me to get 11. he warned me to avoid Marble Arch as there was going 12. he told me to hold the ladder as it was . . . I suggested tying/advised him to tie as it was much safer 13. he told them to read . . . and not to write 14. he warned me not to leave my money 15. he advised me to open 16. he invited her to lunch that day. She said she'd love to but she was afraid she couldn't leave 17. h warned me not to take more than two of them 18. I asked to speak to Albert/ asked if I could speak . . . She said he was . . . I asked her to wake him as I had 19. he advised me to buy 20. they said I was being exploited and that I ought to leave my job/and advised me to leave 21. she told them to fasten their . . . as there might be 22. he warned me not to drive . . . or oncomin drivers might take me 23. he asked to see my licence 24. I advised him to swee up 25. she said the bathroom was empty and asked me to put . . . when I had 26. he reminded me to insure my 27. she begged him not to . . . and reminded him that they had to 28. I urged Tom to go . . . before his toothache got 29. he advised me to cut my hair as/saying that I would find 30. he asked for

Exercise 15

1. the clerk asked me to fill up the form 2. he asked me to read 3. she asked for a new cheque book. He asked her to show him her 4. Tom says that we are to be ready/should be ready 5. he begged me not to tell his mother 6. he ordered us not to fire/warned us not to fire 7. he advised me to take 8. she asked me to help her 9. he warned me not to drive 10. he warned/ told/advised me not to smoke 11. she said that when I'd chosen a book I was to bring it to her and she would 12. he told me to show 13. a notice warned/ ordered us to reduce speed at once 14. he asked to see my ticket 15. he warned me to keep an eye on my luggage as the place was 16. he said that when I'd read it I was to pass it on *or:* he told me to pass it on . . . when I'd read it 17. he ordered me to stand 18. he told me to press the button whenever I saw . . ./he said that whenever I saw . . . I was to press

19. he told her to sit down and tell him what was worrying her 20. he told
me to walk . . . and just to nod if I recognised my attacker but not to say/
and said that if I recognised my attacker I was just to nod but not to say
21. he said that even if I felt hungry I wasn't to/shouldn't eat . . ./he advised
me not to eat . . . even if I felt 22. he asked Ann to ring and order a taxi
for him. She suggested (his) going/advised him to go by tube as it was . . .
23. she suggested buying some yeast and making their own bread as the
bread they were getting was 24. he advised them to boil the water (first) if
they had to use it, and warned them not to drink it unboiled 25. he suggested
not telling anyone/that they shouldn't tell anyone till they were . . . report
was 26. Tom says he's got the tickets and (that) we're to meet him . . .
27. he urged the strikers to show that they were . . . He urged/asked every
man when the vote was taken 28. A notice advised customers to count their
. . as mistakes could not 29. he warned me not to clap yet, as she hadn't
finished. He added (that) singers loathed people who clapped 30. he reminded
me to put my name

Exercise 16

1. Paul wants me to get him 2. Mr White would like you to meet him
3. Ann offered to get . . . Mr Jones said he'd rather she got . . . Ann said
there weren't any and (that) the shops were 4. he told me not to worry . . .
as he made . . . I asked if he learnt from his . . . or if he kept 5. I said I was
looking for . . . who drank in that bar, and asked the barman to point him
out to me when he came in. The barman advised me to keep away from
Albert as he didn't like strangers 6. He asked to have a look at my paper/
asked if he could have . . . as he wanted to see . . . I said I hadn't . . . and
asked him to wait . . . He said he couldn't wait long as he was getting
7. she said we had woken (*or:* woke) . . . the previous night and that we
must try . . . that night. I promised we would 8. he complained that the
soup was cold . . . and asked why he never had . . . She explained it was
because the kitchen was . . . If he insisted on . . . he must/would have to
put up . . . He suggested getting . . . She said (that) she wouldn't 9. he
said my licence was . . . I admitted that it was but said I had applied . . .
He warned me next time to apply . . . before my present one had expired
10. I said I'd have the money for him the following . . . and asked if I should
post it to him. Tom asked me to keep it in my safe till he could come . . . a
lot of his mail had been going astray lately and he would hate to lose one of
my 11. he asked to borrow my map/asked if he could borrow my map. I said
he was always borrowing it and advised him to get/suggested his getting/
asked why he didn't get one of his own 12. he said that when we heard . . .
we were to shut and go *or:* he told us to shut the windows and go downstairs
when we heard . . . I asked what we were to do/should do if the stairs were
blazing 13. she asked if I heard the noise and what I thought it was. I (said
I) thought it was . . . but she (said she) thought it was . . . and asked me
to go/advised me to go/said I'd better go 14. they told Ann it was her turn
. . that night. She protested that it couldn't be as she (had) babysat the
previous night and the night before that, and she was only supposed . . .
they begged her to do it just that once and promised not to ask her to do
any the following week 15. he said it was the best . . . problem was that they
expected . . . The tourists asked why he had brought them there. He told
them not to get excited as he kept ties . . . in their predicament, and he
asked what colour they would like, adding that the ties were 16. I suggested
starting/offered to start/asked if I should start the next day. Tom said he'd
rather I started that day 17. I advised her to go and see the film as it might
help her . . . Ann pointed out that the film was 18. he said he saw/had seen
. . . and one of them (had) sat up and waved to him. I asked which of them
(had) waved. He said he didn't know; he wasn't/hadn't been near enough

19. I asked what (had) caused . . . He said she must . . . but he couldn't understand . . . the wreck was 20. she said her car wouldn't start. The battery was flat. She asked them to give her a push just to start her . . . Bill advised her to sell the car. Peter said nobody would buy it and suggested putting . . . Jack said they'd give her . . . but told her to check that there was petrol . . . and reminded her 21. he said he'd been given . . . that he'd have to . . . I suggested (his) throwing . . . and saving himself . . . (or: I advised him to throw . . . and save himself) 22. he told me to press . . . I said that last time he had told me to press . . . He said that that had been 23. Tom told me not to brake if I found myself skidding as that only made . . . He advised me to try . . . skid. I said I knew what I should do but that when I started . . . I got . . . that I did. On hearing this Jack told me to stop and let him . . . as we were just coming . . . and he didn't wish 24. he said he'd run out . . . and asked if I'd got any. I said I hadn't but offered to go out and get some/but said I'd go out . . . if he liked. He told me not to bother as he'd missed 25. he said that repairs to cars rented from them must be arranged through their office. So if anything went wrong with the car I'd hired I was to ring . . . on my card. The office was open . . . I asked what I should do if something went 26. I asked why he hadn't . . . He said that they had signalled but that she had come (or: came) on in and had run (ran) aground. I asked what was going . . . He said they were going . . . but that if they didn't get . . . she would be there till she broke up, and there'd be 27. I asked why he was spending . . . on the accounts. He said he couldn't . . . he seemed to be . . . and that meant he'd have to . . . of his own money . . . I asked if he'd like me to go through them and see if I could . . . He said he wouldn't, but he'd like me to lend him 28. I asked (Jack) why he was looking so . . . He said he'd just asked . . . and she'd refused. I said I thought she preferred . . . and advised him to cut his hair and shave off his beard 29. she asked how he (had) got up the tree. He said he (had) used . . . but that someone went/had gone off . . . he was sawing. He told her to go . . . and not just stand 30. He asked if I was ill and I said that I wasn't. He asked if I'd slept well the previous night and I said that I had. Then he asked/wanted to know why I was sitting . . . were working, and told me to go out . . . and give 31. he asked/told passengers . . . to go . . . Peter advised Mary to go . . . but said that he'd have to . . . He said he'd take . . . than she would and asked her to wait for him 32. Tom says that we aren't to worry about him. He wasn't badly . . . and is being . . . He says he's coming back next Wednesday . . . and wants us to meet the plane 33. he asked what he was to do with his . . . She advised him to put . . . but warned him not to put . . . or they'd go hard 34. he suggested driving on . . . and trying . . . I asked what he would do if that was . . . He said we'd just . . . as it would be 35. she said they had . . . but that he was . . . wouldn't hear me . . . I asked what I was to do/should do if he woke up. Ann told me to give him some of the biscuits if he started growling. I asked how she knew he liked those . . . She assured me that all dogs liked them. It said so 36. he warned me that if I even touched . . . alarm bells would ring . . . and I would be . . . I asked if he was . . . He told me to try it and see.